Contents

Introduction	4
Using the air	6
Hot air balloons	8
Kites	10
Paper darts	12
Gliders	14
Getting off the ground	16
Nature's living propellers	18
Helicopters	20
Wings of many parts	22
Secrets of bird flight	24
Wings shaped for a purpose	26
Changing direction	28
Proving that people can fly	30
The early flying machines	32
Flying faster than sound	34
Jumbo journeys	36
Flying by computer	38
Hovercraft	40
Flying into space	42
Satellites	44
New words	46
Index	48

Introduction

propellers
page 16

gliders
page 14

kites
page 10

hovercraft
page 40

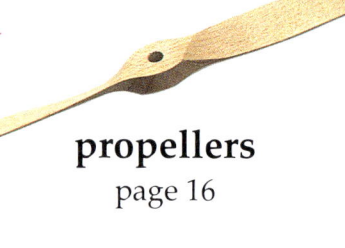

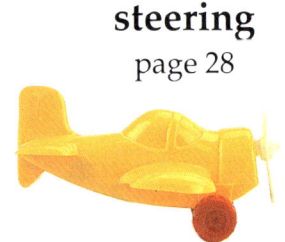

steering
page 28

giant jets
page 36

birds
page 24

lift
page 6

early flight
page 32

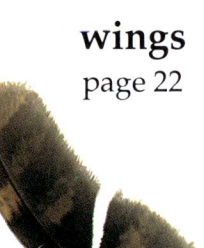

wings
page 22

Look out of the window and see the birds and insects flying about. Watch the seeds of dandelions floating along on the breeze or the winged sycamore seeds spinning to the ground. Watch a cricket match and see the bowler make the ball fly through the air. Look high in the sky and see aircraft cruising above the clouds.

Flying makes it easy to move quickly from place to place and to explore new areas or to get high above the ground and see the world. But flying for people is a luxury. For other creatures it is a way of surviving.

Insects were the first creatures to take to the air. They began to fly over 300 million years ago and they are still the most common flying creature.

wing shapes
page 26

balloons
page 8

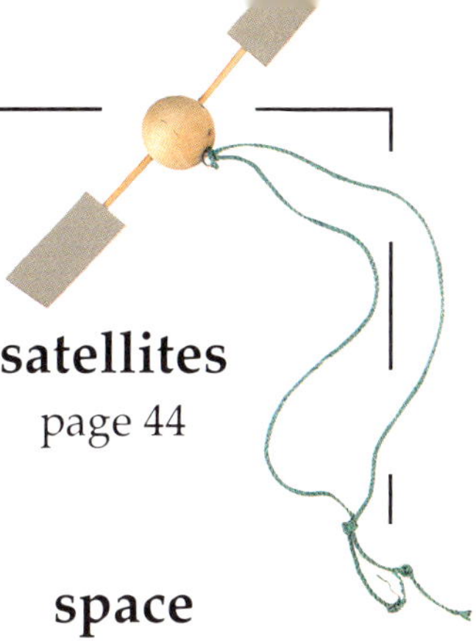

satellites
page 44

space
page 42

Icarus
page 30

insects
page 18

About 150 million years ago insects were followed into the air by huge reptiles called pterodactyls, a kind of flying dinosaur.

The first true birds flew over fifty million years ago. Since this time they have been kings of the skies.

The only mammals to fly under their own power are the bats. Bats have special skin that spreads between the fingers of their hands and their tails.

People are newcomers to the skies and they are still the most clumsy. Where birds, bats and insects can take off and land easily, people need to build machines to help them along.

In this book you can discover the fascinating ways to fly in any way you choose. Just turn to a page and begin your discoveries.

helicopters
page 20

darts
page 12

supersonic
page 34

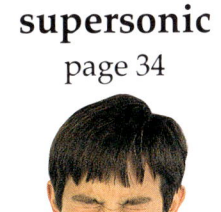

computers
page 38

Using the air

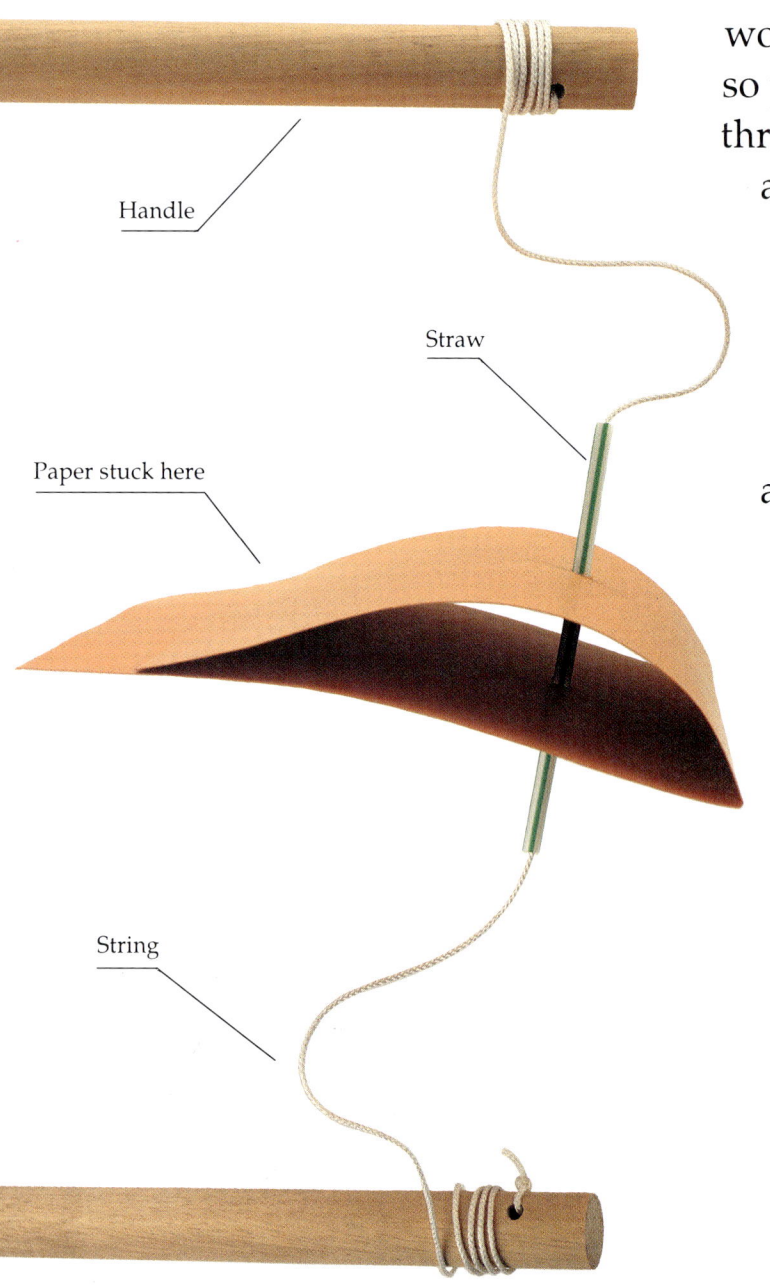

Handle

Straw

Paper stuck here

String

Just as people who wade through water find it hard work pushing the water aside, so people who walk or cycle through the air have to battle against it. They cannot fly. But swimmers move in a way that uses the water. Swimmers can go fast because the water works for them, not against them. In the same way, flying happens when the air works with the fliers, not against them.

Getting the lift
Flying happens when the air is made to cause enough upward movement (called **lift**) to balance an object's weight.

You can easily make a model aeroplane wing from a piece of stiff paper and see how it gives lift. Fold the paper in half and then slide the top half so that it buckles up. Glue it in this position. Pierce the paper and

Air resistance
To find out about the way air can be made to work for you, hold a board in front of you and run about. Feel how the air pushes harder against the board the faster you move.

Try angling the board down. This gives an upward pressure on your arms; you are starting to make the board lift – but not yet enough to fly!

Hold the string taut like this before you make your wing fly

push a short straw through the holes as shown here.

You need two wooden handles and a piece of string. Thread the string through the straw and tie it to the handles. Hold the handles so the string is upright then move the wing through the air quickly and see what happens. You can have a competition to see who can get the wing to lift the highest.

Hot air balloons

When you sit before an open fire you can see smoke, sparks and small flecks of ash wafted up in the invisible currents of hot air. They are in fact 'flying' on these hot air currents.

One of the first ways people tried to fly was by trapping some hot air inside a bag. Underneath the bag, or balloon, they tied a basket for passengers. This became known as a hot-air balloon.

Up, up and away
Modern hot-air balloons are made of thin flimsy material such as nylon.

To get enough lift to carry passengers the balloon has to be the size of a house. It is filled with hot air from giant gas burners.

A balloon drifts with the wind and cannot be steered. Most balloons are flown at dawn or dusk when the air is still and the balloon will travel smoothly through the air.

Pin

Bead

Make a hot air detector
To make a hot-air detector, copy this circle on to a piece of thick aluminium (cooking) foil. Cut out the circle and then very carefully cut along the lines. Push a pin through the centre and put a small bead on the pin. Ask a grown-up to fix the pin to a short stick.

Twist each piece of the foil until it looks like the picture. If you hold this rising air detector by the stick over a hot table lamp or a central heating radiator it will soon start to spin as the warm air rises through the blades.

Stick

Shape to cut out of aluminium foil

Bend the disc like this to make the fins

Hot-air detector in action

Source of heat such as a light bulb

9

Kites

Kites are very ancient flying machines. They are simply a sheet of paper or fabric tied to a lightweight frame.

Kites can stay up in the air for a long time if they are controlled properly because the way they are held lets them get lift from the air.

How a kite works
Kites can only be flown when there is a good wind because they work by catching the air.

When a kite flies it makes an angle to the wind. As the wind rushes past, the air going over the top of the kite has to make a longer journey than the air flowing under it. The difference in air flow makes the air press up under the kite and gives the lift.

Kite manoeuvres
To launch your kite ask a friend to throw the kite in the air as though they were throwing a paper dart. As soon as the kite is airborne, pull the control string to make the kite move quickly through the air. This will give it the lift to go higher.

Try making the angle to the wind very steep. Your kite will not catch the wind properly, **stall** and then sink to the ground.

Use the control strings to change the angle of the kite in the wind. With practise you can make a kite soar up and dive down, or bank sideways

Lift

Direction of air flow

Weight of the tail helps to keep the kite angled correctly to the wind

Controller

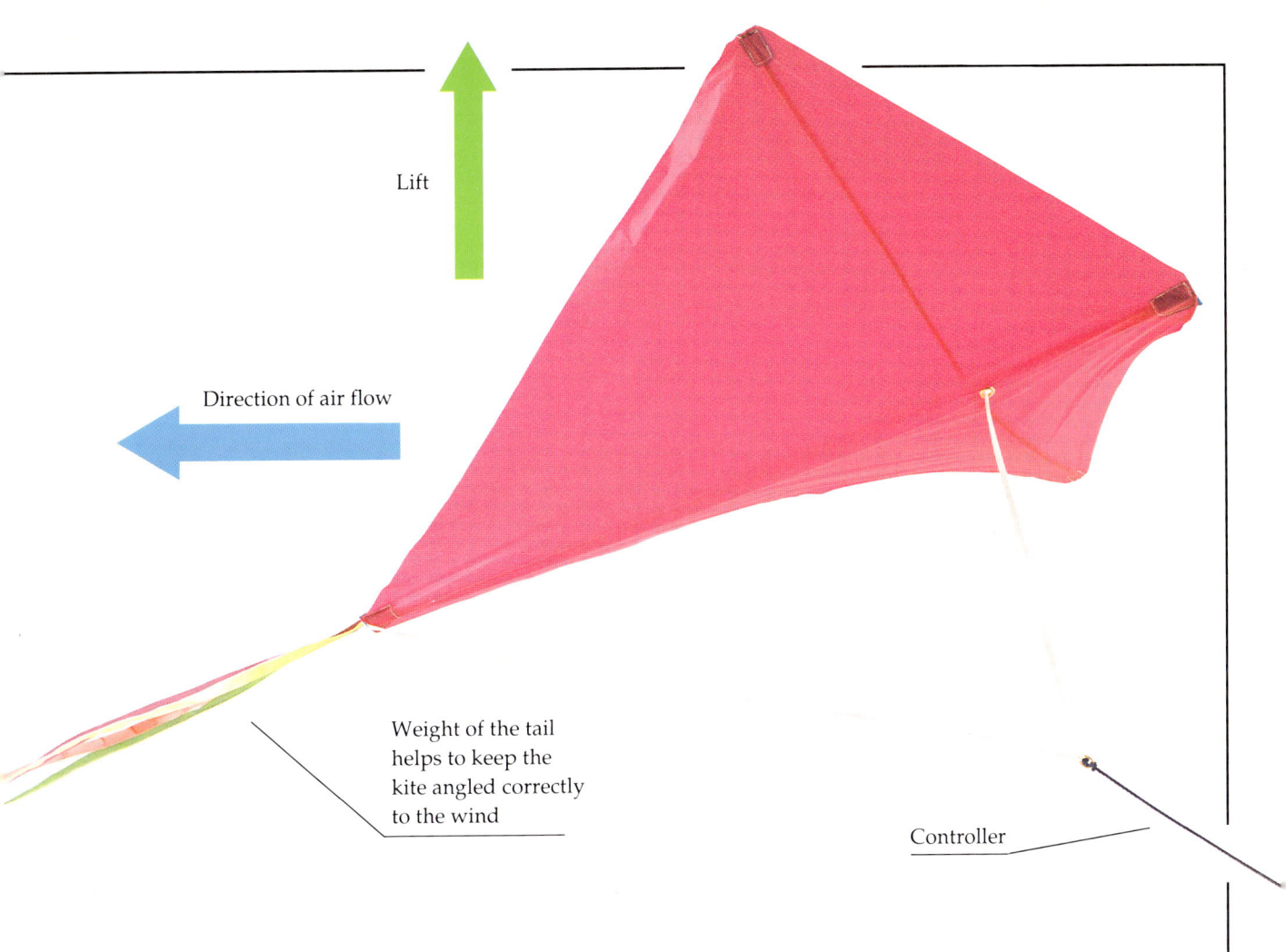

Hang gliders

Hang gliders are shaped like giant kites. Most of them are arrow-head (delta) shaped with a frame made of aluminium and covered with nylon.

The pilot is held beneath the frame in a harness and he steers the kite with a control bar.

To get a hang-glider airborne the pilot must be launched from a high cliff top or a high hill with steeply sloping sides. The pilot runs into the wind and then lifts the nose to split the air flow and get the lift needed to fly.

Hang gliders have travelled over 300 kilometres.

Paper darts

If you throw a flat sheet of paper into the air it will flutter lifelessly to the ground. But if you make it into a paper dart it will travel for many metres.

Paper darts show just how important design and a strong structure are to flying. Some paper darts look like real aeroplanes, others like birds. All of them are gliders and have no power of their own. They rely entirely on their shape to give them the lift that holds them in the air.

Paper aeroplanes
Paper aeroplanes, usually called paper darts, are gliders. There are many variations of the paper aeroplane. The best ones should travel over 5 metres and stay up for over 4 seconds.

The paper aeroplanes shown on these pages are made from a single sheet of standard stiff writing paper.

Launching the dart
Hold the dart like this, tilting it slightly so the tip of the dart points slightly upwards. This will give it the right angle to get the lift from the air when you throw.

If the dart is launched at too steep an angle it will 'stall', come to a stop in the air, and fall to the ground. Each dart is different so experience is the only way to get the longest glide without stalling.

Make your own aeroplanes
You can make any design of aeroplane you want. To find out how good it is just race it against the model on this page. The only rule is that you must use the same size of paper each time. What do the wings on your winning model look like?

Making a paper dart
To make the dart shown here follow the stages below with the pictures. You may find it helpful to ask a grown-up to help you.

6. *Yellow stage.* When you have folded along all the creases the dart will be complete like this and ready to throw. To hold everything in place you may want to put a paper clip on the underside part.

5. *Pink stage.* Open the paper out and, using the creases you have already made, fold the bottom in as shown on the right. The left-hand side shows one more stage of folding along the creases.

4. *Green stage.* Fold as before.

1. *Orange stage.* Take a piece of paper and fold it along the centre.

3. *Blue stage.* Fold again, bringing the folded piece over to the centre line.

2. *Purple stage.* Fold the paper over on itself until the folded piece meets the centre fold.

Gliders

A modern glider is an aeroplane without an engine. It is launched from a towing tractor or a light aircraft and then released when it has gained enough height.

Glider pilots try to find upward moving currents of air to help them gain height. Gliders with skilled pilots can stay in the air for many hours and travel hundreds of kilometres.

Look for gliders circling in the thermal

Thermals

A glider must get enough lift even though it travels at very low speeds. This is done by having specially shaped long slender wings that stand straight out from the glider body (called the **fuselage**).

Glider pilots can stay up almost indefinitely if they get help from rising currents of hot air, known as **thermals**. If you see gliders circling in the air you can be sure the pilots are using the thermals to get a free tow <u>back</u> high in the air so they can carry on gliding.

Strength with lightness

Gliders have to be designed to be strong and lightweight. Many gliders are made from matted glass fibres glued together with special plastics. This material can be moulded to shape and it is also very strong even when thin.

Turning power

Many aeroplanes move themselves through the air using propellers. Another word for propeller is airscrew. Propellers change a round and round movement into a forward one.

The angle of the blade is called the pitch. This propeller has a fixed pitch, but many propellers have blades that can be turned during flight

The never ending screw
Think of a propeller as part of a screw that continually turns in the air. As it turns it pulls its way through the air.
Each turn of the blade pulls air from the front and slides it out to the back. This propeller belongs to a small single-engined aeroplane. The curved shape of the blades can clearly be seen. When the engine is switched on it turns the propeller quickly. When it spins fast enough it will pull the aeroplane through the air.

How a screw works
The long curving thread on a wood screw is the key to how all screws work. When the screwdriver is turned round, the thread pulls the screw straight into the wood.

Make a propeller

Propellers are simple to make from a single sheet of cardboard or thin plastic. If you cut out a large version of the shape shown here and fold it in this special way you will have a windmill. Now you put a long pin through it and stick it to a display board or a stick.

Look at the shape you have made. Try to run your finger through the blades to show the way the air moves. Now blow on the blades and they should turn. The faster you blow, the faster the propeller will turn.

Windmills

It is no accident that the blades of a windmill look like those of a propeller. A windmill is a kind of fixed air-screw. As the wind blows past the blades, they turn and drive the mill.

Pin

Support rod

Nature's living propellers

Insects are rather like living propellers. They were the first creatures to fly. But when you look at an insect with its flimsy transparent wings you wonder how they can fly at all.

Back beat
Wings cut through the air and are twisted to prepare for downbeat

Fantastic energy
Insects have to use an enormous amount of energy to stay up in the air. Even this moth cannot rely on its wings for much gliding help. If insects were to try to glide like a bird they would simply come crashing to the ground.

The power put into wing movements explains why an insect can fly. Weight for weight insects can put far more power into their wings than humans can put into flapping their arms.

Wings on springs

Insect wings are simple flaps attached to the central part of the body called the thorax.

As an insect squeezes in its body the change of shape forces the wings down. Then as the body is relaxed it springs back into shape and this pushes the wings up again.

Fast beat

As the insect moves its wings up and down they actually make a figure of eight shape. An insect's wings therefore pull it off the ground by pushing the air backwards just like a propeller.

This hard work needs high revving 'engine'. Some insects reach one thousand complete wing beats a second. The buzzing sound of an insect is made by the fast beat of the wings.

The insect changes direction by changing the angle at which it beats its wings.

Reverse
Wings now fully forward and twisted

Down beat
Wings pushed forward and down and given a twist

Lift-off
Wings drawn back and up

A living propeller

Most insects use their wings in a similar way to propeller blades. They do not use them like an aeroplane or a glider.

Imagine an aeroplane without a cabin. The pilot sits astride the engine with the propellers just behind his head. Now you can imagine the way an insect flies. This makes them extremely manoeuvrable and explains why they can take off and land so quickly.

Helicopters

A helicopter has a large type of propeller called a rotor. This is fixed horizontally, but the blades can be turned to make the helicopter go forwards or backwards as well as up and down.

Helicopters use the air much like insects. This is why they can turn and twist in the air much better than an aeroplane. But this type of flight also uses up a lot of energy.

The whirring blades
The blades of a helicopter are called the **rotor**. It is difficult to see the blades of a helicopter as they spin round during flight. They have to move so fast because they have two jobs to do. First they must hold the helicopter in the air, and they must also pull it forward.

This is done by tilting the whole blade slightly in the direction the pilot wants to go.

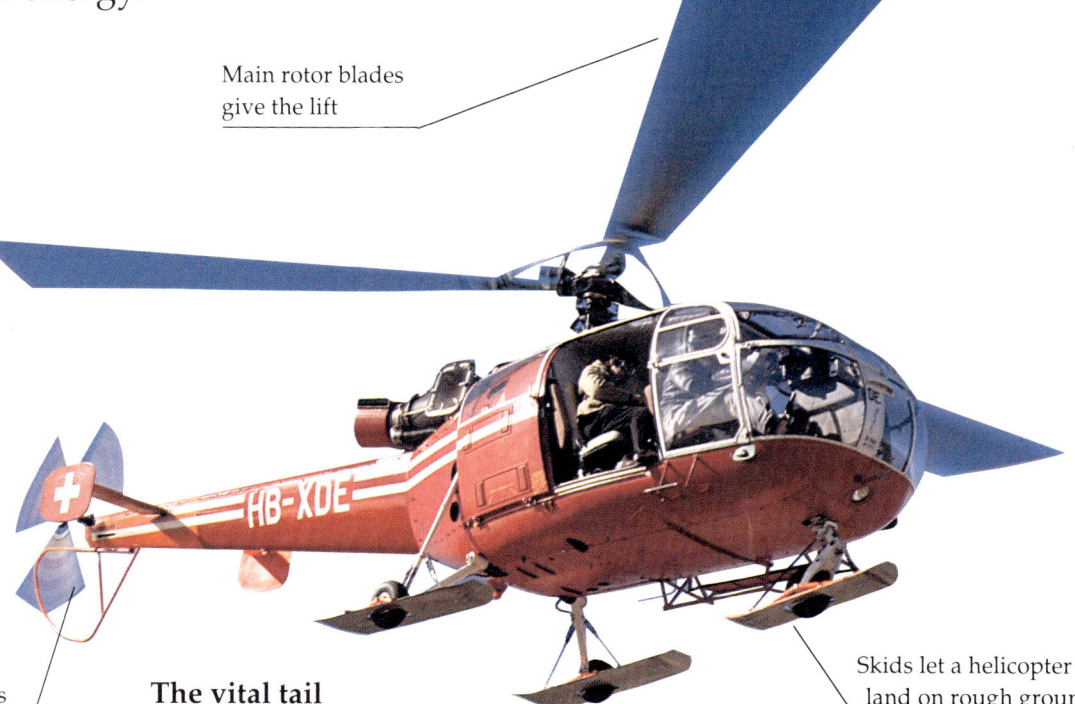

Main rotor blades give the lift

Rear rotor stops the helicopter spinning round

Skids let a helicopter land on rough ground

The vital tail
When the blades of a helicopter are started the turn of the blades would make the helicopter body spin round and round as well.

To stop a helicopter spinning, they have a second rotor. Usually it is in the tail. The rotor does not push the helicopter along. Its job is to balance out the turning motion. So to change direction the helicopter pilot either speeds up or slows down the small rotor.

Make an autogyro

As the helicopter blades spin, so the helicopter lifts off the ground. If a helicopter engine fails the blades will keep turning because the fall causes air to flow through the blades. This effect gives the pilot a chance to land safely.

To see how blades turn round as they fall through the air – called the **autogyro** effect – take a piece of writing paper and tear as shown here. Bend the strips and then add a weight to one of the strips. A couple of paper clips will do. Now hold it high up and let it fall. The rotors will spin as it sinks to the ground.

A model helicopter

To see how a helicopter works you only need a piece of cardboard, a cotton reel a pencil and some thread.

Cut out and bend the shape shown here. This will be the rotor of the helicopter. Then push the pencil through the centre to make the drive shaft.

Now put the pencil in the cotton reel and wind some thread round the pencil.

When you pull the thread fast it will unwind, turn the pencil and the rotor will lift into the air.

Wings of many parts

A bird's wing is a very complicated 'arm'. This is because it does so many different jobs. It has to support the weight of the body during flight and act as a propeller. The feathers have to be self smoothing, cope with knocks and bumps, and they have to be renewable so that they never wear out.

Outer wings
The feathers on this part of the wing – called the **primaries** – are long and often stand out from each other, leaving gaps or slots in between. This pattern of feathers and gaps allows the bird to change direction easily and also take off and land under control.

The outer wings are also used to move the bird forward. Each wing-tip twists during the downward beat, dragging the bird through the air

Feather zippers
The feathers that are used for flying are very special. Not only are they tough, but they can bend and twist with great ease. Look closely at a flight feather and you will see it is made of many long strands. Each of these strands has little hairy hooks right along its length. If the feathers get ruffled by the wind the bird can easily use its beak to zip the hooks up again. Hey Presto, a new sleek finish for efficient flying on the next trip.

Tufts for control
Near the 'wrist' a bird wing often looks as if it has a bunch of feathers out of place. However, these feathers help fine tune the wing during take off and landing

The inner wing
This part of the wing is moved from the 'shoulder'. The flight feathers on this part of the wing – the **secondaries** – are smaller than on the outer wing. They lie close together to make a smooth streamlined shape.

The whole inner wing acts like the wing on an aircraft. It is arched and tilted slightly so that the air flows past the wing in a special way. The effect is to give the bird the lift it needs to keep in the air

This is the wing of an owl

Secrets of bird flight

Birds have thrown all their excess body baggage overboard. They have no teeth or heavy jaws. They have a skull that is the lightest of all creatures. They have feathers that make flexible wings, hollow bones that are very light yet strong, a large strong heart and powerful breast muscles. This gives them a lot of power for a very light body.

Powering muscles
A bird's muscles have to be powerful enough to keep the wings moving for hours on end without tiring. In birds the breast muscles may make up half the body weight. These muscles are matched by an immensely strong heart.

Streamlined feathers
The feathers arch up over the wing in a special way. As they fly through the air the arched feathers produce a **streamlined** effect that lets the bird go through the air with the least effort.

Streamlining allows birds to be the fastest creatures on earth. A Peregrine falcon can reach nearly 300 kilometres an hour as it dives after its prey – about the same speed as the world's fastest express train.

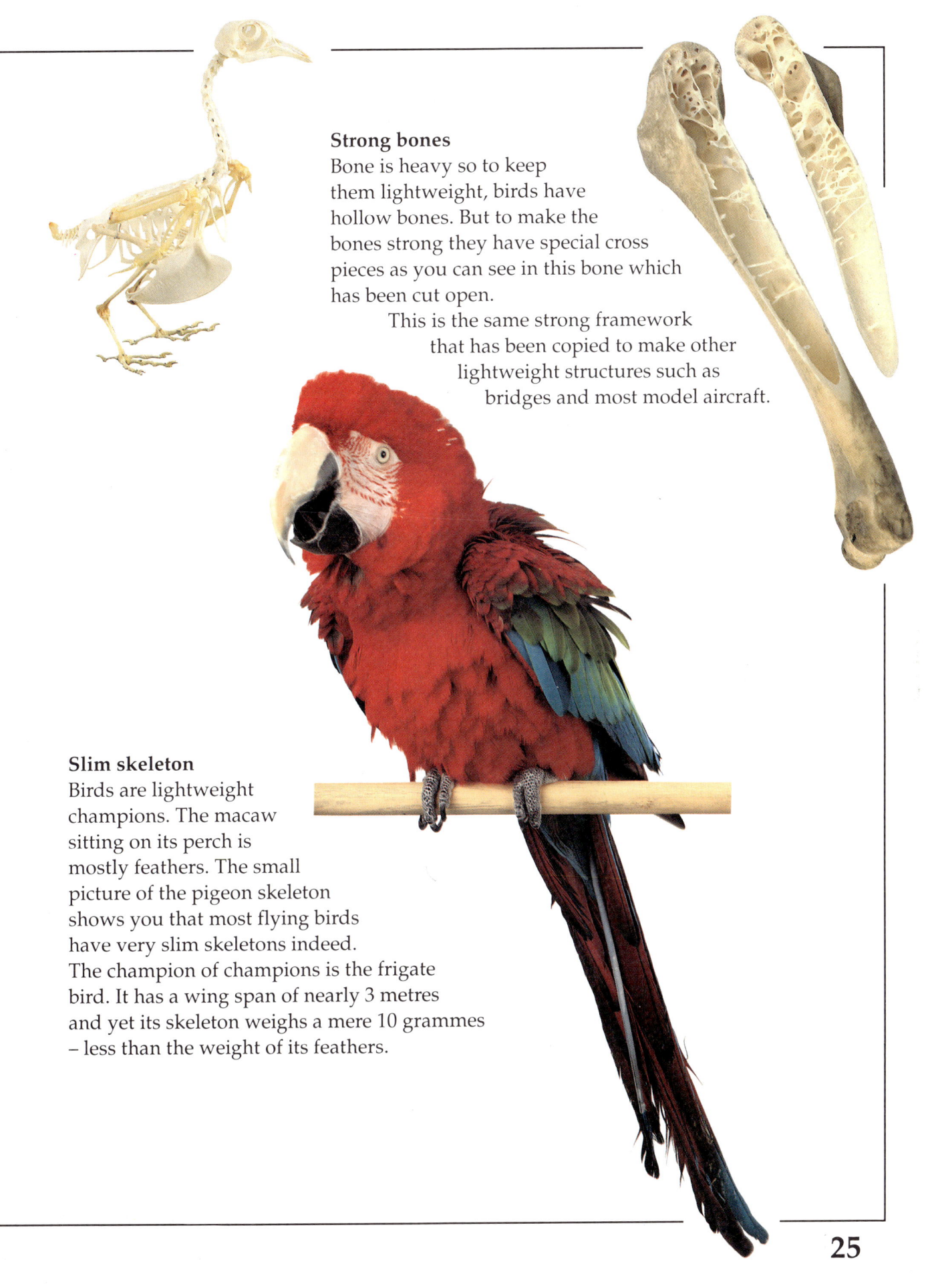

Strong bones
Bone is heavy so to keep them lightweight, birds have hollow bones. But to make the bones strong they have special cross pieces as you can see in this bone which has been cut open.
This is the same strong framework that has been copied to make other lightweight structures such as bridges and most model aircraft.

Slim skeleton
Birds are lightweight champions. The macaw sitting on its perch is mostly feathers. The small picture of the pigeon skeleton shows you that most flying birds have very slim skeletons indeed. The champion of champions is the frigate bird. It has a wing span of nearly 3 metres and yet its skeleton weighs a mere 10 grammes – less than the weight of its feathers.

Wings shaped for a purpose

Birds have many types of wings. Each type is matched to the way the bird lives. Long wings are for gliding, while short ones are for quick twisting and turning. Wide wings are useful for hovering while thin wings are best for long distance travel.

Manoeuvring wings
Birds such as sparrows and woodpeckers that live in the forests have to twist and turn among the branches. They also have to take-off and land in very cramped spaces.

Kingfishers are masters of coping with small spaces. They wait on branches that overhang a river, then dive after fish.

Kingfisher

26

Bald Eagle

Soaring wings
Many of the largest birds spend much of their time soaring high into the air, then hovering while they search for their food on the ground below.

Condors, eagles, vultures and owls all have special wings to help them do this. Each wing is long but also wide with many slots between the feathers. This is a good all round wing, helpful for gliding but also very manoeuvrable for quick attack on any prey.

Gliding wings
The longest, slimmest wings make gliding easy for birds like the albatross. These birds can glide for many hundreds of kilometres without landing. They even sleep on the wing. These special features allow albatrosses to fly non-stop round the world.

High speed wings
Long thin wings are best for high speed flight. Migrating birds, that might travel thousands of kilometres each year, have this type of wing.

Long wings do have their disadvantages. They are not suited to short take-offs or landings. Ducks and geese, for example, need quite large lengths of water to use as 'runways'.

Gannet

27

Changing direction

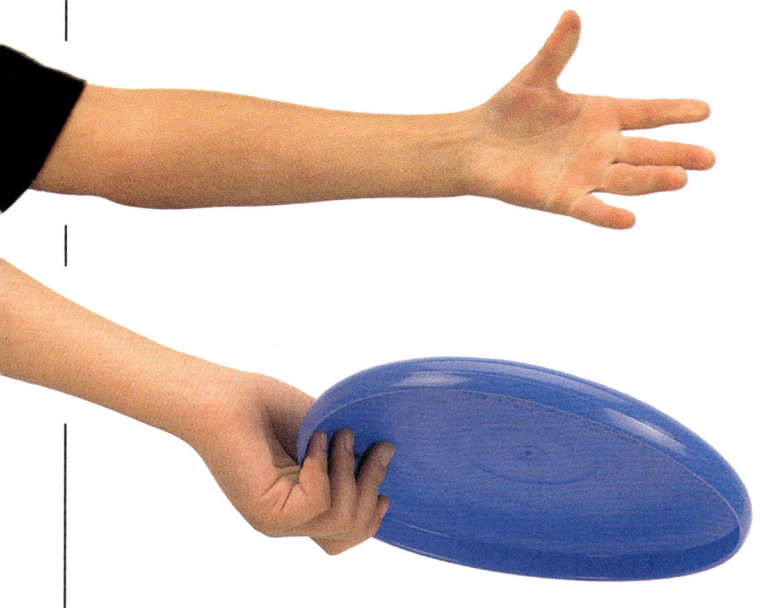

An aeroplane is much harder to control than a car. It can go up and down, go sideways and roll over. Pilots have to keep control of all these directions. To do this they use hand and foot controls.

How wings control flight

A frisbee is a flying machine. The curved edge splits the air and gives lift just like a wing. But the frisbee is not very controllable. If you want to control the flight there has to be some way to change the air flow. Birds do this by changing the shape of their wings and insects change the angle at which they beat their wings.

Aeroplanes are designed more like bird wings with small flaps that let the pilot change the wing shape.

Control a frisbee
Try throwing a frisbee and deciding how it will land. You will find you have little control because a frisbee is a wing without flaps.

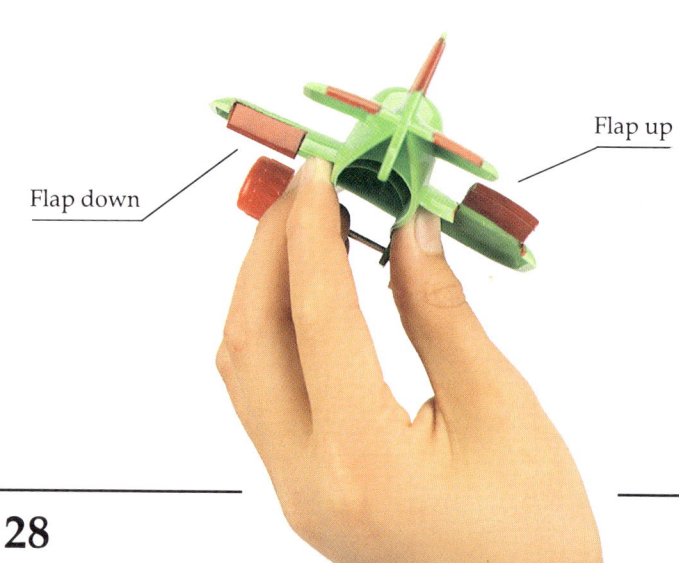

Flap up

Flap down

Rolling
An aeroplane can be made to roll over. Rolling, also called banking, is one way of turning. To bank, the flaps (called **ailerons**) in the wings are operated. One flap is pushed up while the opposite flap is pushed down

28

Flying straight and level

Most aeroplanes are designed to fly straight and level on their own. This is achieved by the special design of the wings.

The best shape for a self-flying wing is flat underneath but arched at the top. It is thick and rounded at the front but tapers to a thin wedge at the back. It is widest where it joins the body and slightly swept back.

Aeroplane steering

To make an aeroplane change direction you disturb the air flow over the wings or tail.

The airflow is disturbed by means of little flaps on the wings and the tail. These can be moved by the pilot using controls in the cockpit. As each control is operated it moves a flap which sticks out and disturbs the air, causing a small change in air flow.

Each type of movement has a special name. The main movements are called, rolling, pitching and yawing.

Pitching

An aeroplane can be made to dive or climb. This is called pitching. Pitch is controlled by the pilot using the control column. This operates the flaps (called **elevators**) in the tail. As the elevators are moved down, the nose dives. When the elevators are moved up the nose climbs

Yawing

An aeroplane can be turned by using the rudder. This is called yawing. Normally an aeroplane is turned by using a combination of yawing and rolling

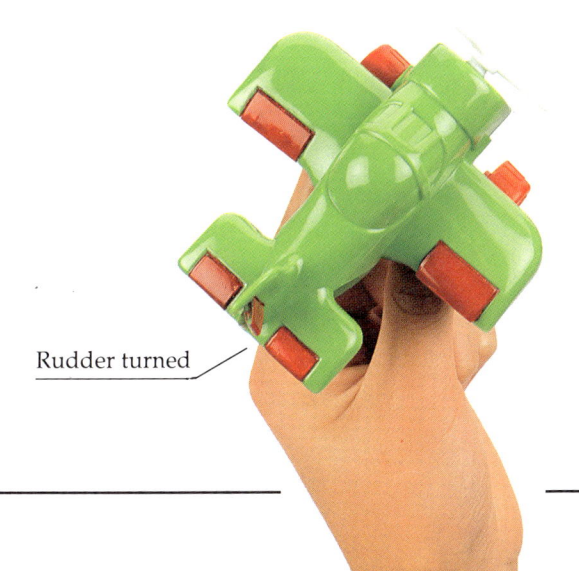

Elevators down

Rudder turned

Proving that people can fly

People are not built to fly. They have heavy bones and their muscles are too weak. But this has not stopped them wanting to power their own aeroplanes.

With special materials and a lot of trial and error, people have at last discovered how to fly using muscle-power.

The story of Daedalus

There is a story in Greek mythology about the first people ever to fly. It is a story that has inspired people to try to fly up to the present day.

In Ancient Greece the inventor Daedalus was said to have been imprisoned along with his son on the island of Crete.

Daedalus built wings of feathers and wax so that they could fly to freedom across the sea. But Icarus was so fascinated by the power of his wings that he grew reckless and flew too close to the Sun, melting the wax of his wings. He crashed into the sea and perished.

Daedalus, who flew more slowly and carefully, made the journey to the distant island safely.

The first aeroplane to fly with muscle power

The first aeroplane to complete a specially designed course for human flight was called the Gossamer Albatross.

The Gossamer Albatross had a wing-span of nearly 30 metres yet because of its extremely light frame and covering it weighed only 27 kilogrammes (half the weight of the pilot). This meant that a single person was able to fly across the English Channel, a distance of 32 kilometres. The pedal-powered aeroplane Daedalus 88 now holds the world record with a flight of 120 kilometres in Greece. It flew at over 18 kilometres an hour.

Getting the lift

If people are to fly they must make the very best use of the air. This means they must design an aeroplane which gives the most lifting power and yet is very light weight. The way to do this is to build broad slim wings like a glider and make them from the newest strong lightweight materials.

The strongest human muscles are in the legs. The best way to power an aeroplanes is with propellers that are turned by pedal power, just like a bicycle.

Compare the successful Daedalus 88 in the picture above, with the traditional way of trying to fly, shown in the picture below. It shows that people can fly – if they use the help of Science.

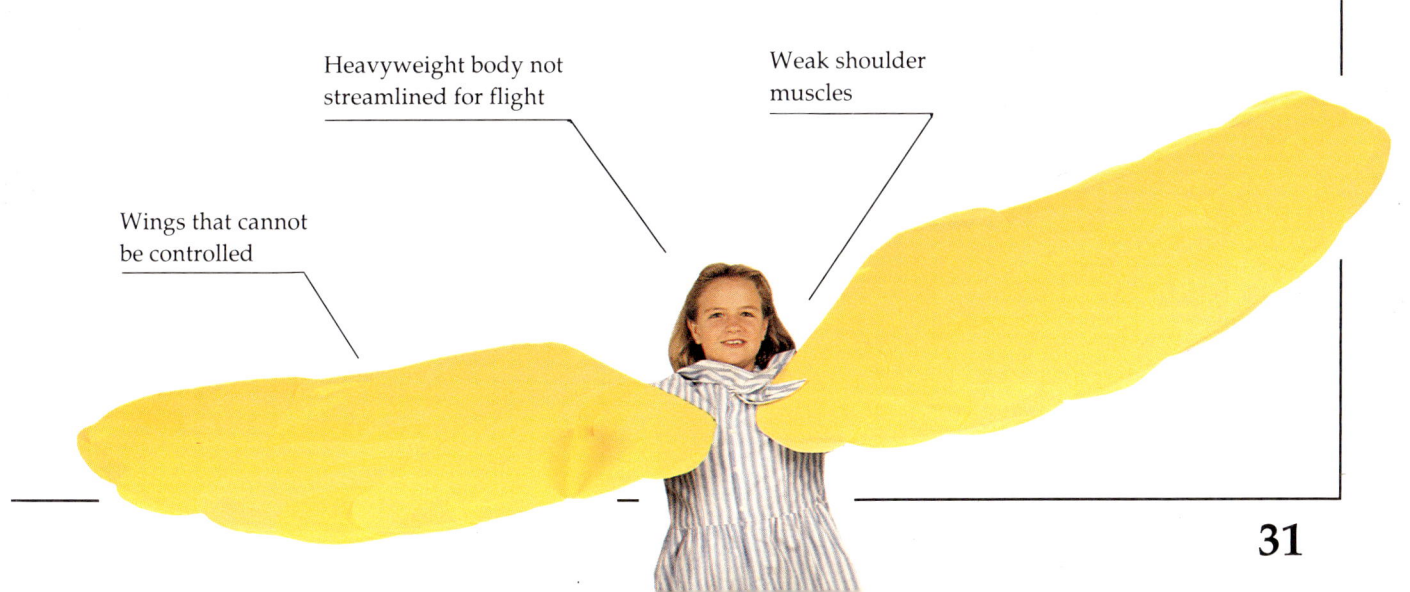

Heavyweight body not streamlined for flight

Weak shoulder muscles

Wings that cannot be controlled

31

Early flying machines

The first people to fly did not have any experience behind them. They had to make the best judgement they could and then use the aeroplanes to test out their ideas. Even today people are still pushing flying to the limits – although they now call on the help of computers.

Working out what to do
Aeroplane flying belongs to this century. In 1903 the Wright Brothers in the USA flew their aeroplane for 12 seconds. They had created history.

To find the right wing shape for controlled flight they had to experiment with over 200 designs. To power the flying machine they used a modified car engine. It had to be made especially lightweight.

Fresh air
The early aeroplanes did not have a cabin. The pilot sat near the wings in an open cockpit. Any passengers sat on seats behind the pilot.

As the aeroplanes became faster and they flew higher, they reached altitudes where the air was thin and cold. From then on the pilot and passengers had to be placed inside a pressurised and heated cabin.

Biplanes and monoplanes

Many early aeroplanes had two wings – one above the other. The biplane wings were easy to make rigid because they could have bracing struts all along their length.

Eventually the single winged aeroplane – the monoplane – was built. The wings were held rigid by a rod (or spar) which went through the aeroplane from one wing tip to the other. Single winged aeroplanes can travel faster and they are more manoeuvrable that biplanes and so nearly all the world's modern aeroplanes have a single wing.

Dog fights

The First World War made a big difference to the history of flying. The opposing sides both made great attempts to make faster and more manoeuvrable aeroplanes.

The best designs were worked out by trial and error. As each new design was tried the air force measured its success by the number of pilots who survived the air battles or dog fights.

This flying helmet and goggles belonged to a pilot who fought in the Second World War. It was needed because the planes did not have pressurised cabins

Stepping stones to flight history

1783	The Montgolfier brothers rose off the ground in a hot air balloon.
1783	Lenormand was the first person to use a parachute.
1852	The world's first airship was launched.
1903	The Wright Brothers make the world's first powered flight.
1909	Bleriot crosses the English Channel in a single seater aeroplane.
1919	Alcock and Brown make the first transatlantic flight.
1927	Lindberg makes the first solo transatlantic flight.
1947	The **jet** engine is invented.
1954	The first vertical take-off aeroplane takes to the air.
1969	Concorde makes its first flight.
1970	The first jumbo jet flies.
1986	Voyager makes the first round the world non-stop powered flight.

Flying faster than sound

Flying fast has always been a challenge to aeroplane makers. Their target has been to travel faster than the speed of **sound**. As a result supersonic aeroplanes were developed.

Aeroplanes need powerful engines and special wings to make them travel very fast. Most high speed aeroplanes look like paper darts. Their shape is like the way the fastest birds hold their wings when they dive.

The sound barrier
When aeroplanes fly very fast they catch up on the sound waves of their engines. This is known as the **sound barrier**.

You do not hear the approach of a aeroplane that is flying faster than sound. The only thing you hear is large bang as the aeroplane goes past.

Concorde
Concorde is the name of the world's only passenger aeroplane that can fly faster than the speed of sound. To achieve this speed Concorde has been built to a shape unlike other passenger aircraft.

To fly fast Concorde has wings that are swept back into a triangle shape. There is no separate tail.

The engines of Concorde are set into the wings so they do not stick out into the air and cause drag.

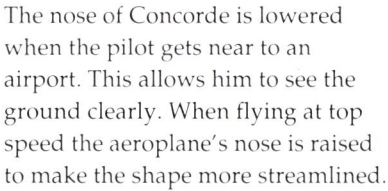

The nose of Concorde is lowered when the pilot gets near to an airport. This allows him to see the ground clearly. When flying at top speed the aeroplane's nose is raised to make the shape more streamlined.

Changing wings

The fastest aeroplanes in the world have wings that change shape. When they are taking off or landing, they need to travel slowly. For this broad long wings are needed. But when the aeroplane moves very fast it is best to have wings that are short and set back more like the flights on an arrow.

The 'swing-wing' aeroplanes solve this problem by having wings that are hinged. As they go faster, the wings change angle and become shorter and more swept back. The position of the wings is controlled by a powerful computer in the pilot's cockpit.

Jumbo journeys

A modern aeroplane has to carry people swiftly, it has to be comfortable and it has to be very safe. Here you can see the major parts of a large passenger aeroplane – one of the most complicated machines ever built.

The body
The cigar-shaped body (fuselage) has to be a comfortable place for people and it has to hold a lot of cargo.
  A platform across the aeroplane separates the passenger compartment (above) from the cargo (below)

The wings
The wings are long, thin and swept back slightly to make the aeroplane more stable at high speeds.
  The wings carry both the fuel tanks and the engines, so they have to be immensely strong

The engines.
Most large aeroplanes use jet engines. A jet engine works by mixing air with fuel. A spark ignites the mixture explosively. The spent gases shoot out of the back of the engine and give the thrust to push the aeroplane forward.
  Some jet engines have 'propeller' blades inside the housing. They are called turbines and they are used to make the engines even more powerful. This allows jet aeroplanes to carry both large numbers of passengers and large amounts of cargo

Keeping comfortable
A modern aeroplane travels at great heights where the air is thin and cold. This is why the passenger compartments have to be heated and kept pressurised.

The flight deck
The pilots control the aeroplane from the area called the flight deck at the front of the aeroplane. Many of the controls can work automatically and are controlled by computers

The landing gear
The wheels used for take-off and landing are stored in the aeroplane body during flight. As the aeroplane approaches a runway the landing gear are lowered and locked in position.
  The force of landing soon makes the tyres wear out. The brakes cannot stop the aeroplane on their own. All the wing flaps have to be lowered and the engines put into reverse to bring the aeroplane to a stop

37

Flying by computer

Many aeroplanes are so complicated the pilot needs the help of computers. Computers make regular checks of the aeroplane and tell the pilot that everything is working properly. Computers can also fly the plane automatically.

In a busy airport computers are vital to follow all the aeroplanes as they land and take off.

On the flight deck
The nerve-centre of a plane is the pilot's flight deck. In this picture you can see the mass of instruments that tell the flight crew about every part of the aeroplane.

Computers make frequent automatic checks to make sure every part of the aeroplane is working properly. Just in case one computer should fail there are always back-up computers to take over automatically.

Airport handling
Modern airports are very busy places. The skies above airports have many aeroplanes that are landing and taking off. Without computers it would be impossible to keep track of every aircraft.

Airports use an echo sounding system that sends out radio waves and then picks up the bounced signals. The system is called **radar** (radio detection and ranging). Each of the signals is fed into a computer and used to give a picture of all the aircraft in the sky. This picture is vital to allow the airport controller to give pilot safe landing and take-off instructions.

Autopilot
On long journeys computers can be used to fly an aeroplane entirely automatically. They will make sure the speed is correctly adjusted to keep the aeroplane flying straight and level even in rough winds.

Air traffic control
Even when they are far from an airport, pilots cannot rely on seeing other aircraft and they need help to fly safely in crowded skies.

Every aeroplane is tracked on a special screen using long distance radar. An air traffic controller uses this information to give each pilot instructions for a safe journey.

Hovercraft

A hovercraft is an extraordinary flying machine. The idea of a machine that can fly and yet move over rough land has produced many types of hovercraft. Here are some of them.

Make a 'hovercraft'

To make a simple hovercraft you simply need two pieces of thin cardboard, a paperclip and some glue.

Cut once piece of cardboard to make a shallow box. Use the glue to fix the sides together. Next make a tube of cardboard and use the clip to hold it. Do not use glue. Put the tube inside the hole in the box and let the tube get bigger until it is a tight fit in the box lid.

All you have to do now is to blow into the tube and the 'hovercraft' will lift and move easily over a table.

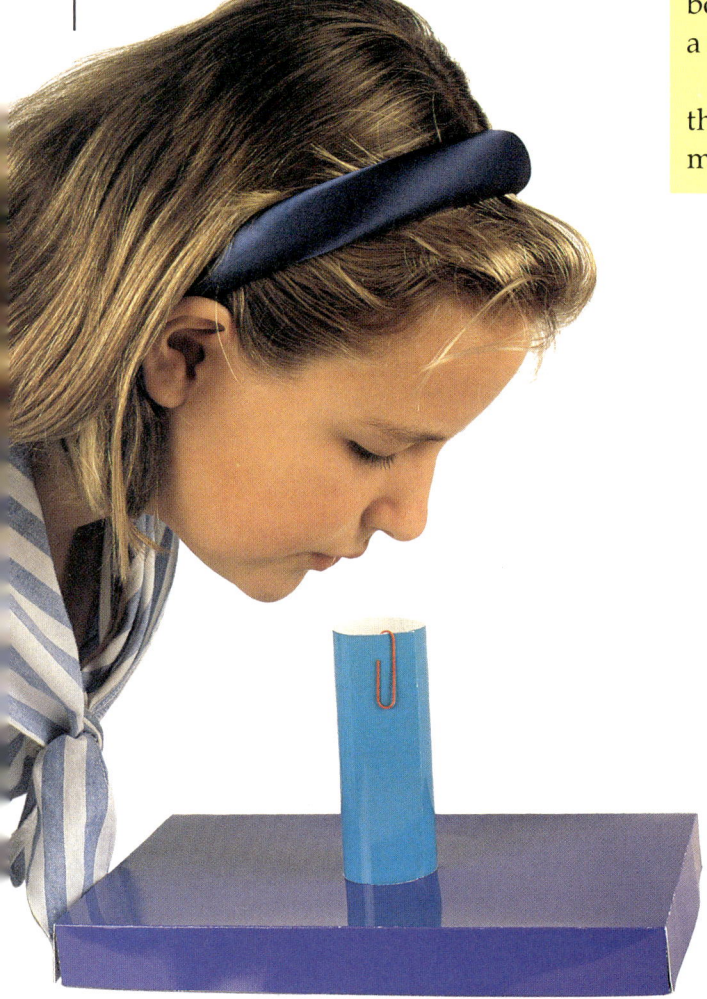

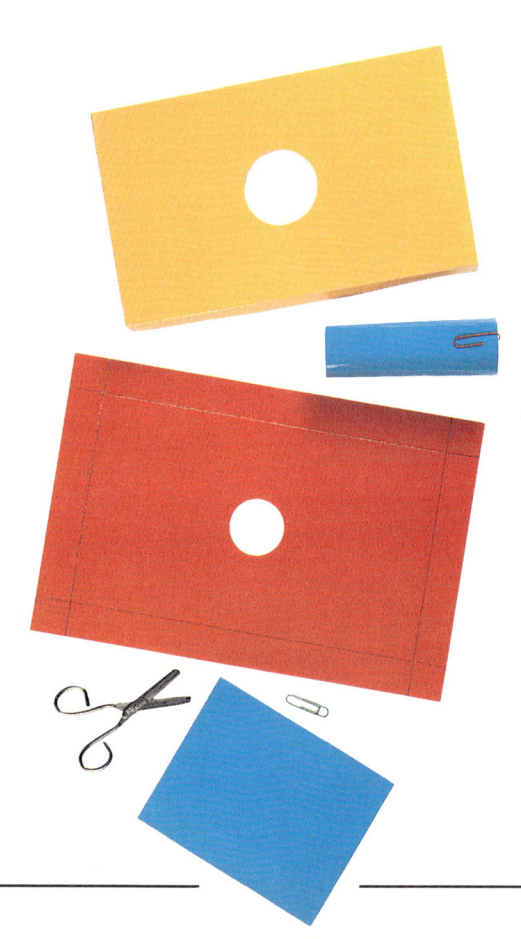

How a hovercraft works
Hovercraft support themselves on a cushion of air. Air is blown in at the top of the machine and this causes the pressure to build up until it takes the weight of the craft.

Around the base of big hovercraft, such as those used for carrying people, there is a black rubber 'skirt'. This allows a hovercraft to move over rough surfaces without too much air leaking away from the machine. On big hovercraft propellers are used to move the machine about.

A hovermower
The motor spins and pulls air into the top of the box. When enough air has built up under the box it lifts a little from the ground. The box also houses a spinning cutting blade.

You do not need to be strong to cut a lawn with a hovermower because the weight of the machine is supported by the air

Flying on water
Hovercraft are used as ferries because they can travel at twice the speed of a ship. They have enough lifting power to carry up to 200 people and their cars. Their speed and flexibility also make them ideal rescue craft.

Flying into space

Rockets are like powered arrows. They are designed in a pencil shape so they will fly through the air as easily as possible.

A firework uses gunpowder as a fuel to propel itself high into the sky. In space there is no air so rockets also have to carry their own supply as big tanks of liquid oxygen.

A modern firework

- Cap
- Propellant
- Guide stick
- Fuse
- Head contains special effects material

Return to earth

Spacecraft are very expensive. The most recent spacecraft, such as the Space Shuttle, are designed to be reusable. They have wings like an aeroplane so that at the end of its mission they can glide back to the earth.

Space shuttles are sent into **orbit** strapped to a rocket. When the main rockets have done their job the shuttle's booster rockets take over and send the craft to its final destination. The engines are fired again to get the shuttle back on course for re-entry to Earth.

The Space Shuttle has a very special covering made from **ceramic** (baked clay) tiles. These can withstand the terrific heat and protect the shuttle and its pilots as they re-enter the Earth's atmosphere.

Caution

This firework has been opened carefully by experts to show the contents. Never open fireworks yourself. Never play with or light fireworks unless you are being supervised by a grown-up

The US Space Shuttle

Both the USA and the USSR have forms of space shuttle. The plan is to use the shuttle as a sort of space-age truck, carrying goods to and from space. It has a cabin near the front and small engines at the back, but the rest of it is a vast cargo bay.

Space design

In the future, space stations will be built from pieces that have been carried into space by space shuttles. When they are built these stations will have no kind of streamlining. In space there is no air and even the most clumsy looking shapes will fly easily.

Although they may be able to fly enormous distances through space, these space craft will never be able to return to the Earth.

This is a space machine of the future. It is called the *Space Sail*. It is designed to move only in space

43

Satellites

Satellites are machines in space that fly in circles round the Earth. They are used for many tasks. Some look down on the weather, some carry telephone and TV signals round the world and some even spy on other countries.

Exactly balanced
Satellites whirl round the Earth in a never ending circular path or orbit. It is as though they were tied to the Earth by some invisible cord.

When you whirl a ball round and round on a thread it is the thread that stops the stick from flying away. As a satellite whirls round the Earth it is held in place by **gravity**.

At a certain distance from the Earth gravity and the 'flying away' force exactly match and the satellite will stay flying round the Earth. This is called the orbit.

Stick with cardboard panels glued on

Satellite made from table tennis ball. (Do not use hard wood)

Thread for whirling the satellite round

Make a satellite
You can see how a satellite works by tying a piece of string very firmly to a ball.

First make sure there is no-one near to you who could be hurt by the swinging satellite. Swing the ball round your head and watch it lift off. It is held in place by the string. The 'string' for a satellite is the Earth's pull of gravity.

What satellites are used for

Satellites have aerials so they can send and receive radio signals. A signal bounced off a satellite can span great distances. Satellites in orbit over the North Atlantic Ocean are used to bounce telephone conversations from Europe directly to North America. There are similar satellites orbiting over the Pacific Ocean to link America with Australia and Japan.

If you telephone a friend in a distant country your voices will be sent out into space and bounced off a satellite.

Satellite power

Satellites do not need any power to stay in space. But their computers do need power and their batteries are recharged using sunlight. The large flaps on this satellite are solar panels used to make electricity from sunlight.

New words

ailerons
these are the flaps that can be lifted from the trailing side of the main wings. They are the flaps you see in use if you travel by air and look from the cabin windows. Pilots use them for changing direction and also for slowing the plane as it comes in to land

autogyro
this is a machine that has freely spinning rotor blades. It is driven forward by a propeller. The forward movement of the machine causes the rotor blades to turn and this gives lift. It is not as manoeuvrable as a helicopter

ceramic
a special kind of clay that has been baked hard. Most kitchen tiles are ceramics. They are hard and brittle, but they can stand up to great heat and they are therefore useful in a space craft when it flies back through the Earth's atmosphere

elevators
these are small flaps in the tail. Even small changes in the tail, will make a big change in direction of the aeroplane. This is why both the elevators and the rudder controls are placed in the tail

fuselage
the name given to the body of the aeroplane. The fuselage is usually cigar-shaped and it is braced to take the weight of the wings and tail

gravity
the force that pulls everything on Earth towards the centre. You can find out much more about gravity in the Science in our World book 5, Falling

jet
this is a form of engine which works by igniting an explosive mixture of air and kerosene (a form of petrol). The process is similar to the way a car engine works, but the exhaust gases are used directly to drive the aeroplane through the air. Jet engines work best at high altitudes, which is one reason aeroplanes fly as high as possible, often at about 13 000 metres

lift
the force that carries a flying object upwards when it moves through the air quickly. It was discovered by an Italian scientist named Bernoulli. He found that a wing split the air in a special way as it went fast through the air and that this difference caused the wing to lift upwards

orbit
the path that a flying object makes as it goes round the Earth. Many satellites orbit the Earth from pole to pole, a few orbit the Earth at the same speed as the Earth turns.

radar
the equipment used to find planes in the sky. A radio signal is sent out from a transmitter. When it reaches a plane or other solid object some of the waves are bounced back and detected by a receiver. The time it takes for the signal to go out and come back gives the position of the plane

rotor
the name given to the long thin blade set that is fitted to the helicopter. Rotors have special joints at their centre which allow the pilot to change the angle of the blades

satellite
an body that is trapped in a roughly circular path by the gravity of a larger body. The Earth and other planets are satellites of the Sun. The Moon is the Earth's largest satellite. Most satellites, however, are small machines sent into space to orbit the Earth

sound
a sound is caused when there is a rapid disturbance in air. It may be produced in the throat to give speech or singing, or it may be due to some other movement such as a loudspeaker vibrating or a balloon exploding

sound barrier
the speed at which a flying object catches up with the sound waves that it produces. People have use the sound barrier as a goal when designing faster and faster planes. The sound barrier is reached at a speed of 322 metres per second

stall
this is the steepest angle that a wing can get lift. If the angle of the wing gets steeper the lift will disappear and the wing will no longer be able to keep the body in the air. Stalling can be a major cause of aeroplane crashes

streamline
a streamlined shape is one that has been shaped to give the least drag as an object moves. It is particularly important that fast moving objects, such as aircraft, are streamlined

thermal
the rising current of air that allows gliders and birds to get lift. Thermals are strongest on a clear day when the Sun can warm the ground. As some places warm faster than others the air above them warms fast as well. This warm air then becomes light and starts to float upwards, creating a thermal

Index

aeroplane 28-9, 32-3, 36-7
ailerons 29
air flow 11
air traffic control 38
airship 33
albatross 27
Alcock and Brown 33
autogyro 21, 46
automatic pilot 39

Bald Eagle 27
balloon 8
banking 29
biplane 33
bird 22-27
Bleriot 33
buzzing 19

ceramic 42, 46
cockpit 29
computer 38-9
Concorde 33, 35
condor 27
control cabin 37

Daedalus 31
dart 12-13, 34
dog fight 33
duck 27

elevators 29
engine 36

feathers 22-3, 24
flying machine 32
frisbee 28
fuselage 14, 36, 46

gannet 27
geese 26
glider 12, 14-15
gliding 26, 27
Gossamer Albatross 30
gravity 44, 46

hang glider 11
helicopter 20-21
hot-air balloon 8
hot-air detector 9
hovering 26, 40-1

insects 18-19

jet engine 33
jumbo jet 33, 36-7

kingfisher 26
kite 10-11

landing gear 37
Lenormand 33
lift 6, 11, 12, 14, 30, 46
Lindberg 33

macaw 25
monoplane 33
Montgolfier 33

orbit 43, 44, 46
owl wing 22-3

pigeon 25
pilot 32
pitching 29
primary feathers 22
propeller 16-17, 18
pterodactyl 5

radar 39, 47
rocket 42-3
roll 20, 29
rotor 2 0, 47

satellites 44-5, 47
screw 16
secondary feathers 23
skeleton 25
skirt of hovercraft 41
sound 34, 47
sound barrier 34, 47
space 42-4
Space Shuttle 42-3
sparrow 26
stall 10, 47
streamline 24, 35, 47

thermal 15, 47
turbine 36

vertical take off plane 33
Voyager spacecraft 33
vulture 27

windmill 17
wing 22-23, 26-7, 33, 36
woodpecker 26
Wright brothers 32, 33

yaw 29